Animals in Their Habitats

Desert Animals

Francine Galko

Heinemann Library
Chicago, Illinois

Designed by Ginkgo Creative
Printed and bound in the United States by Lake Book Manufacturing, Inc.

07 06 05 04
10 9 8 7 6 5 4 3 2

Library of Congress Cataloging-in-Publication Data

Galko, Francine.
    Desert animals / Francine Galko.
        p. cm. — (Animals in their habitats)
Includes bibliographical references (p.   ).
Summary: Describes deserts, the different kinds of animals that can be
found in them, and their ecological importance.
    ISBN 1-40340-178-0 (HB), 1-4034-0435-6 (Pbk.)
    1. Desert animals—Juvenile literature. [1. Desert animals. 2. Deserts. 3. Desert ecology. 4. Ecology.] I. Title.
    QL116 .G25 2002
    591.754—dc21

                        2001007654

Acknowledgments
The author and publishers are grateful to the following for permission to reproduce copyright material:
Cover photograph by Thomas Wiewandt
p. 4 M. Freeman/Bruce Coleman Inc.; p. 5 Martin W. Grosnick/Bruce Coleman Inc.; pp. 6, 9, 14, 19 Thomas Wiewandt; p. 7 Lynn M. Stone/Animals Animals; p. 8 Willard Luce/Animals Animals; p. 10 TC Nature/Animals Animals; p. 11 Linda Bailey/Animals Animals; p. 12 Ted Levin/Animals Animals; p. 13 Robert P. Carr/Bruce Coleman Inc.; p. 15 Joseph Van Wormer/Bruce Coleman Inc.; pp. 16, 18 Alan Blank/Bruce Coleman Inc.; p. 17 Jeff Foott/Bruce Coleman Inc.; p. 20 Dwight Kuhn; p. 21 Bob and Clara Calhoun/Bruce Coleman Inc.; p. 22 Kenneth W. Fink/Bruce Coleman Inc.; p. 23 John S. Flannery/Bruce Coleman Inc.; p. 24 David Liebman; p. 25 Gerald and Buff Corsi/Visuals Unlimited; p. 26 OSF/Animals Animals; p. 27 D. Lyons/Bruce Coleman Inc.; p. 28 Lee Foster/Bruce Coleman Inc.; p. 29 Bayard Brattstrom/Visuals Unlimited
Every effort has been made to contact copyright holders of any material reproduced in this book. Any omissions will be rectified in subsequent printings if notice is given to the publisher.

Some words are shown in bold, **like this.** You can find out what they mean by looking in the glossary.

To learn more about the stinkbug on the cover, turn to page 9.

Contents

What is a Desert?

A desert is a kind of **habitat.** Deserts are very dry places. It usually does not rain a lot in a desert. It is often very hot during the day and very cool at night.

Some deserts have almost no plants at all.
Other deserts have unusual plants, such as
cactuses. Cactuses need very little water.
Most desert plants and animals use little water.

Where are Deserts?

Deserts are all over the world. They form in places where the air is very dry and there are few clouds. There is little rain if there are no clouds.

Some deserts form near mountains. Tall mountains keep rain clouds away from deserts. The mountains make a **rain shadow.** This means that the rain falls on the mountains instead of in the desert.

Desert Homes

Many desert animals live under the ground. Others live under rocks and near plants. The **cactus** wren makes its nest inside a cactus.

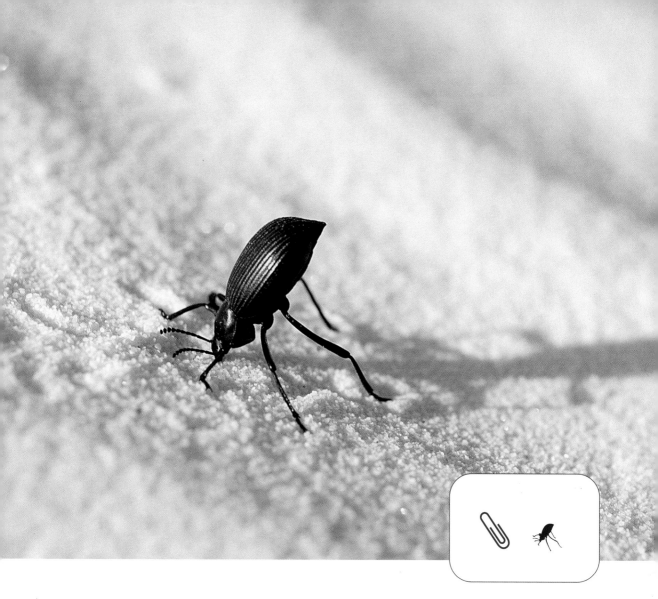

Stinkbugs live in the ground and on rocks. If you scare a stinkbug, it will spray a stinky liquid at you. It might also stand on its head.

Living Underground

Many desert animals go underground
sometimes. The sun can't get in and it's
cool. Desert tarantulas make their homes
underground. They spin **silk** to fill their nest.

The burrowing owl lives under the ground.
It often stands in front of its **burrow** during
the day.

Living Among the Rocks

Some desert animals live on or under the rocks in the desert. Bighorn sheep live on rocky desert mountain sides. They eat small plants, even **prickly cactuses.**

The western diamondback rattlesnake hides under rocks most of the day. The diamond shapes on its back blend in with desert rocks.

Many desert animals need desert plants. Elf owls make their nests inside **cactuses.** They often live in a hole that has been left by another animal.

Pack rats make their homes among **prickly** pear cactuses. The prickly plant **protects** them from coyotes and other **predators**. Pack rats also eat the prickly pear fruit.

Living in Puddles of Water

Rain and water from under the ground can **ooze** up through the ground. This makes puddles. Desert dragonflies begin life as **larvae** in these puddles of water.

Desert pupfish live in the warm, salty water of Death Valley. In the summer, most of the water dries up and many, but not all, of the pupfish die.

Gila monsters can go a long time without eating. They store food as fat in their tail. They are not really monsters. They are lizards. Gila monsters eat small desert animals and their eggs.

Desert tortoises eat plants. They like desert grasses and flowers. They get all the water they need from the plants they eat.

Living with Little Water

Scorpions have a hard shell that helps keep water inside their body. During the day, scorpions sometimes **burrow** into the dirt to escape the sun.

Kangaroo rats sleep underground during the day. They come out at night when it's cool. Kangaroo rats can go their whole life without ever drinking.

Desert Predators

Some desert animals are **predators.** They hunt other animals in the desert. This red-tailed hawk eats rabbits, mice, snakes, and even other birds.

Coyotes hunt rabbits, mice, and other animals at night. You might hear coyotes howl at night in the desert. During the day, they live in **burrows** in the ground.

Hiding a in Desert

Camouflage is one way to hide from predators. Hackberry butterflies begin as caterpillars in desert hackberry shrubs. The caterpillar's head looks like it has hackberry thorns on it.

Texas horned lizards sometimes lie flat and still against the ground. It's hard to see them when they do this. Their spots and **spines** blend into the rocky sand.

Desert Babies

Baby roadrunners stay in their nest for twenty days. Then they jump out and run around with their mother. She shows them how to catch insects, snakes, and lizards to eat.

Baby western coral snakes hatch from eggs.
A mother western coral snake usually lays
only two or three eggs.

Protecting Desert Animals

When people move to the desert and build homes, they take away places for desert animals to live. Sometimes, people bring new plants to the desert. They try to make the desert green.

This harms the desert animals and plants that already live there. Desert animals like this sidewinder snake can lose their homes. Leaving deserts alone helps protect the animals that live there.

Glossary

burrow to dig under the ground. It is also an underground home.

cactus desert plant that needs little water

camouflage way an animal hides itself

den animal's underground home

habitat place where an animal lives

insect small animal with six legs

larva (more than one are called larvae) very young insect

ooze to move slowly

predator animal that hunts and eats other animals

prey animal that is hunted and eaten by another animal

prickly has sharp points

protects keeps safe

rain shadow the side of a mountain that does not get much rain

reptile group of animals that includes snakes, lizards, and turtles

silk string-like material that a spider makes and uses to spin a web

spine horn-like part of an animal's body

More Books to Read

Arnosky, Jim. *Crinkleroot's Guide to Knowing Animal Habitats.* New York: Aladdin Picture Books, 1998.

Fowler, Allan. *It Could Still Be a Desert.* Danbury, Conn.: Children's Press, 1997.

Silver, Donald M. and Patricia J. Wynne. *Cactus Desert.* Columbus, Ohio: McGraw-Hill, 1997.

Index